THE PRINT BOOK

By **HANNAH TOFTS**
Written and Edited by Diane James
Photography by Jon Barnes

CONTENTS

Scholastic-TAB Publications Ltd.
123 Newkirk Road, Richmond Hill, Ontario, Canada

Here are some of the things you will need to start printing. Almost anything with a raised surface will give a print so look for different textures. Wood off-cuts are useful for making printing blocks.

You can use almost any paint for printing but oil paint gives the best results. If you use oil paint you will need a good supply of rags and turpentine for cleaning up.

Look for flat surfaces to roll your paint on for printing – glass, linoleum or the shiny side of a piece of panelling are best.

block of wood

tape

craft knife

cardboard and paper

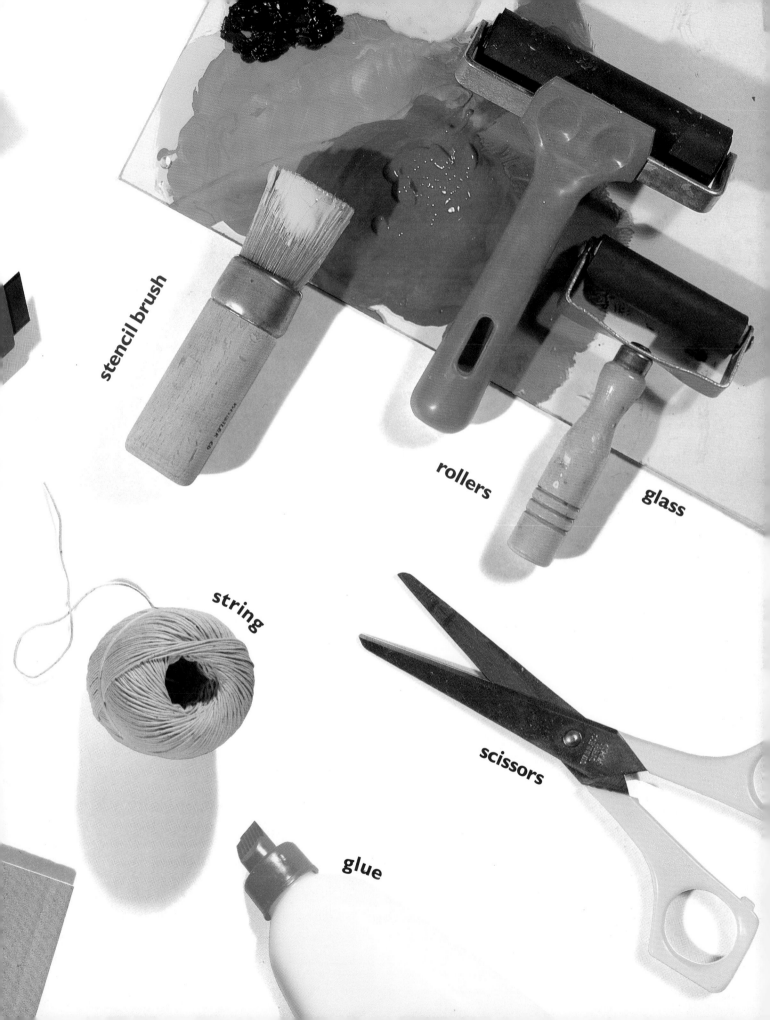

stencil brush

rollers

glass

string

scissors

glue

Start printing straight away with things you can find in your own home or at school. Look for objects with interesting shapes. Cut fruit and vegetables make good prints.

Cover the objects with thick paint and press them firmly onto a sheet of paper.

Experiment by building up patterns and overlapping shapes. Try printing wet paint on top of wet paint to get a different effect.

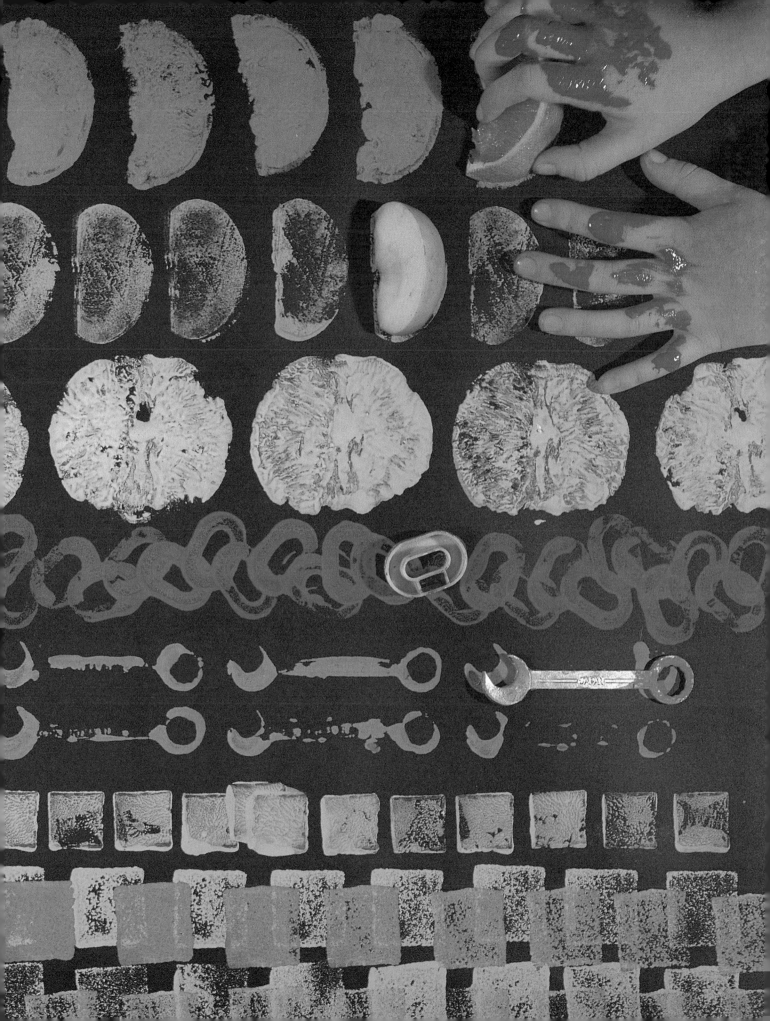

You can take a print from most things that have a textured surface – rough, knobbly or patterned. Look around both indoors and outdoors for different textures.

You will have to cover the object that you want to take a print from, with paint. Make sure you will not be doing any permanent damage and, if in doubt, use paint that will wash off easily.

Use thick paint and a large brush or roller to cover the surface you want to print from. Lay a sheet of paper over the object and press down firmly and smoothly or run a clean roller over the paper. Lift the paper off gently and leave your print to dry. Try experimenting by combining different textures.

The prints above were made from a rough plank of wood, a car tire, a man-hole cover and knobbly glass. The ones on the left were made with blocks of wood and leaves.

Here are some suggestions for making simple printing blocks that you can use over and over again.

Using an old rolling pin, wrap string round and round and glue the ends firmly. Mix some fairly thick paint on an old piece of glass, linoleum or panelling (shiny side). Roll the rolling pin up and down the paint to coat the string. Make a print by rolling the rolling pin smoothly along a piece of paper.

You can make other printing blocks by gluing string onto a block of wood in a pattern. Or, you can wind thick cord round a block, or stick on lengths of broken pasta. Try taking more than one print before covering the block with paint again.

Think of ways you could use
your printed papers – wrapping
paper, covering books or even
as wall paper!

These printing blocks are easy to make and give good, strong prints.

Use pieces of thick cardboard for the printing blocks. From another piece of cardboard, cut straight strips using a craft knife. Glue the strips onto the printing block to make a pattern.

Cover the printing block with fairly thick paint using a roller. Press the block firmly onto a sheet of paper and smooth over with a clean roller.

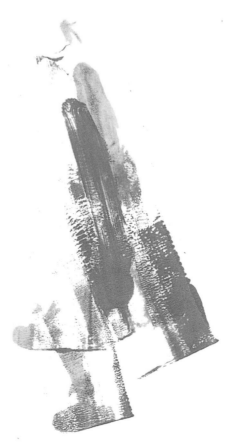

Try using strips of torn paper or thin cardboard instead of straight strips. Make two or three blocks in the same way but use different colours of paint to print each one. See how many different patterns you can make by alternating the colours.

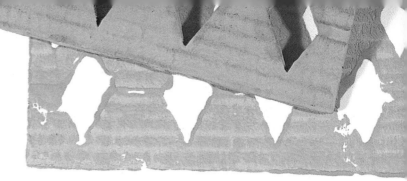

These printing blocks are made by cutting shapes out of pieces of cardboard. Cut two rectangles from an old cardboard box using a craft knife.

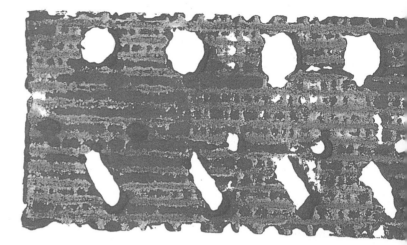

Cut shapes from one of the pieces of card – diamonds, triangles, squares and rectangles. Cover the cardboard with fairly thick paint and make a print. Now, cut shapes out of the other piece of cardboard. You will be printing this piece of cardboard on top of the first print, so try to use shapes that will work well. Use a different colour to print the second block on top of the first.

After a few experiments, you will discover that you can use the white spaces left to make interesting shapes.

Here is a method for making several prints of the same picture. First, make a colour drawing and then trace it off.

Cut a separate piece of cardboard – the same size as your tracing – for each colour that you want to use. Lay your traced drawing on one of the pieces of cardboard and trace off all the objects that are the same colour. Do the same for each colour on separate pieces of cardboard. Now trace all the objects onto a separate sheet of cardboard and cut them out. Glue the cardboard shapes in position on the sheets of cardboard. These are your printing blocks.

Make cardboard corners like the ones in the big picture. Tape them down so that your printing blocks fit into the corners exactly.

Lay a sheet of paper – the same size as the printing blocks – in the cardboard corners. Roll paint over one of the printing blocks. Place it carefully over the sheet of paper using the cardboard corners as a guide. Press down and lift off. Repeat this process with each of the different colours.

Try building up a picture using printed shapes! Cut shapes from stiff cardboard using a craft knife. Use a strip of cardboard as a handle. Fold it in half and bend back the two ends. Stick the ends firmly to the back of your cardboard shapes. Cut up old cardboard tubes and use the edges to print curves. Use thick paint and watery paint to get different effects. Try overprinting shapes while they are still wet.

Make a stencil by cutting a shape from a piece of stencil board, or heavy cardboard. Place the stencil on a sheet of paper and use a stencil brush – with short, stiff hairs – to stipple the paint on.

You can use the shape cut from the stencil to make a print. Lay the shape on a piece of paper and splatter paint over it. Use a nail brush or an old toothbrush and a piece of cardboard to splatter with. Always splatter away from you!

Try making this pattern by laying cardboard rectangles on a piece of black paper and stippling over them with white paint. Re-position the rectangles and stipple over with yellow paint.

Try experimenting with different shapes to build up your own patterns.

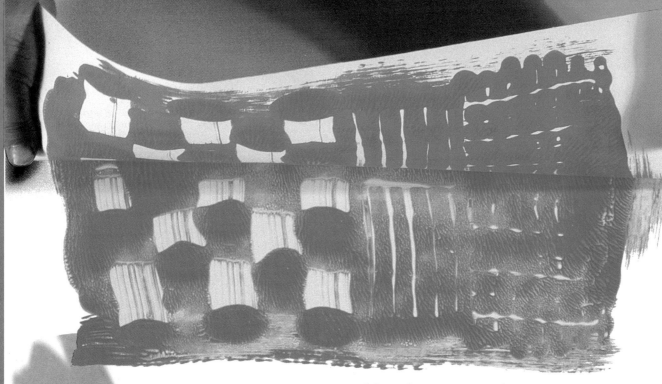

You do not need any printing blocks or cardboard shapes to make a monoprint! You need a smooth surface such as a piece of glass or linoleum. Some kitchen table tops can be used but make sure the paint will wash off afterwards.

To make a pattern like the one above, cover the flat surface with fairly thick paint. Use a piece of cardboard to scrape away patterns from the paint. Lay a sheet of paper carefully over the pattern. Smooth the paper gently with your hand. Peel the paper back to reveal your print! Try taking more than one print.

Another method of monoprinting is to paint a simple picture straight onto your flat surface. Lay a sheet of paper over the picture and smooth over carefully. Lift the paper off and leave the print to dry.

Here are some more suggestions for monoprinting patterns using cardboard scrapers. Roll thick paint over a flat surface. Divide the paint area into sections and make a different pattern in each area.

Try printing a picture for your wall!
You can use lots of different printing
methods in the same picture but
keep the shapes as simple as possible.
Start with the background and build
the picture up.

Patterns make good pictures too!
Look at the leaf pattern here and try
to work out your own patterns using
different printing blocks and stencils.

Here are some examples of printed papers using methods from this book. Try making a selection of your own designs. You can use printed paper to cover books, to write on, to wrap presents and as pictures for your wall!

You can print on fabric just as easily as on paper. Most craft shops sell fabric paints which will not wash out. Follow the instructions carefully!

Cotton is the best fabric for printing on. See what you can do with a plain handkerchief, or a scarf or T-shirt.

Try making your own writing paper! You can print border designs using simple shapes and you can personalise the paper by printing your name on it! If you want to print your name or initials, try using very simple shapes to make letters. Turn the page and you will find some suggestions for printing your own envelopes.